PARIS OLYMPICS

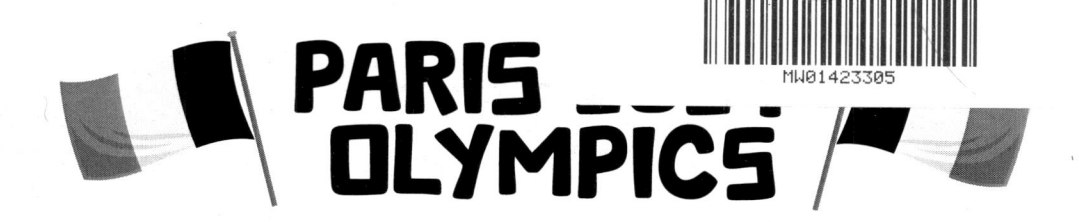

WHO ARE THE OLYMPIC MASCOTS?

The Phryges are the official mascots of Paris 2024 Olympic and Paralympic Games. They are two anthropomorphic Phrygian caps that are a symbol of France.

What does anthropomorphic mean?
It just means an object having human-like characteristics. Here's what the real French hat looks like

WHEN DO THE GAMES BEGIN AND END?

- Torch relay leaves Marseille for Paris: **May 8, 2024**
- Opening ceremony: **July 26, 2024**
- Closing ceremony: **August 11, 2024**.

Follow the relay: www.paris2024.org/en/olympic-torch-relay-route/

The most popular sports are broadcast on television, especially the opening and closing ceremonies. It's meant to celebrate unity via sports with all countries coming together. This time the host is France so you're sure to see the Phyrges there and a few cultural celebrations of France. It's their time to show off what they love so much about their country.

3

15 FUN FACTS ABOUT THE OLYMPIC GAMES

1.) Ancient Olympics, 8th century B.C. to 4th century A.D., occurred every four years until Emperor Theodosius I banned them.

2.) Modern Olympics revived in 1896 in Greece, after about 1500 years.

3.) Ancient Greek athletes competed nude, unconcerned with modern sponsorship or protection.

4.) Ancient games spanned five to six months. Today it's only two.

5.) Women entered the Olympic games in 1900.

6.) Winter and Summer Olympics were synchronized from 1924 to 1992, but now alternate every two years.

7.) Only four athletes have won both Winter and Summer Olympic medals, one achieving this feat in the same year.

8.) 2012 London Olympics Village needed 165,000 towels for two weeks.

9.) Official languages: English, French, plus the host country's language.

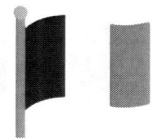

10.) Johnny Weissmuller, a Tarzan actor, won five swimming golds in 1920s.

11.) Artists participated in Olympics from 1912-1948, competing in various artistic fields.

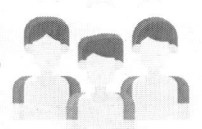

12.) In 1936 Berlin Games, two Japanese pole-vaulters tied for second place. One medal was cut in half, and each man received half a medal.

13.) The Olympic torch ignites at the temple of Hera in Greece, using a parabolic mirror and sun rays.

14.) The torch has traveled by runners in boats, airplanes, and even space shuttles.

15.) The Olympic flame must burn throughout; reignited only with a backup flame from Greece.

12 FUN FACTS ABOUT THE PARIS 2024 OLYMPIC GAMES

1. The Olympic Games Paris 2024 will officially be held from July 26th until August 11th 2024, while the Paralympic Games will take place from August 28th until September 8th. Click here for the full calendar of events.

2. The Olympic competitions for football and rugby at Paris 2024 will begin on July 24th. Two days before the Opening Ceremony.

3. The Olympic Games Paris 2024 take place exactly 100 years since Paris hosted the Olympics back in 1924.

4. Paris will join London as the only cities to host the Olympics three times. The Games were in Paris in 1900, 1924 and now in 2024, while London hosted the Games in 1908, 1948 and 2012.

5. On July 26, 2024 the Opening Ceremony of the Olympic Games in Paris will be held almost exactly 100 years after the 1924 Closing Ceremony, which was held on July 27th.

6. The Paris 2024 Opening Ceremony will not be held in a stadium for the first time ever. Instead it will be done on the River Seine, the river that crosses the centre of Paris.

7. There will be 32 sports played during the Paris 2024 Olympic Games and 329 medal events in total.
8. The sport with the most medals being awarded at Paris 2024 will be aquatics with 49 events across the disciplines of swimming, marathon swimming, diving, water polo, and artistic swimming. Athletics follows closely with 48.
9. There should be about 10,500 athletes present at the Olympic Games Paris 2024. The final number of competitors will be confirmed following the conclusion of the Olympic Qualifier Series.
10. There will be one new sport for the Paris 2024 edition of the Olympics: breaking (or break dancing) Competition in the dance sport will comprise two events — one for men and one for women — where 16 B-Boys and 16 B-Girls will go face to face in solo battles.
11. Approximately 45,000 volunteers will help at the Paris 2024 Games.
12. There will be a total of 35 Olympic venues at Paris 2024, with fourteen sites hosting 24 Olympic sports located within 10km of the Olympic Village.

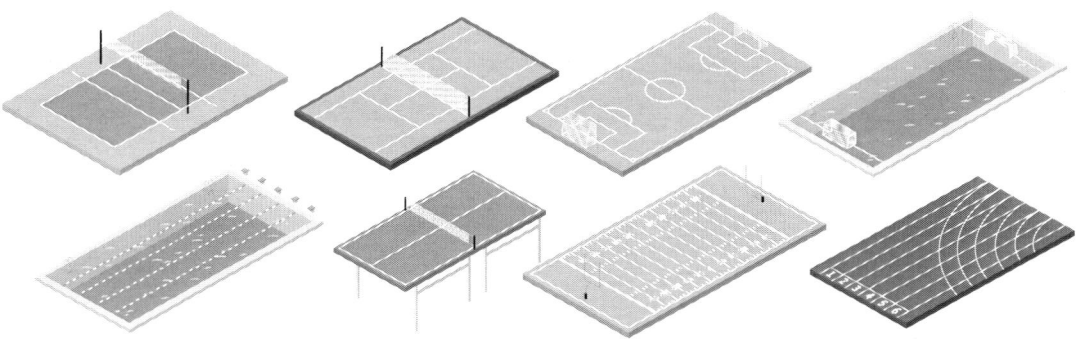

FAMOUS PLACES WHERE SPORTING EVENTS ARE TAKING PLACE IN PARIS AND BEYOND

Eiffel Tower Stadium
- Beach Volleyball
- Road Cycling passes under the Eiffel Tower

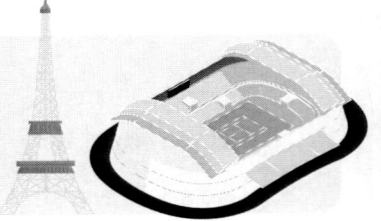

Champ de Mars Arena
- Judo & Wrestling

Grand Palais (palace)
- Fencing & Taekwondo

Marseille Marina
- Sailing

Teahupo'o
- Surfing in Tahiti, French Polynesia

Concorde
- Basketball
- BMX Freestyle
- Breaking
- Skateboarding

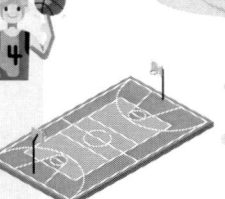

Palace of Versailles
- Equestrian & Modern Pentathalon

Find out more about some of these locations in Andrew & Ashley's European Tours travel guide to Paris!

8

WHERE DOES THE OLYMPIC TORCH RELAY START AND END?

Did you know that weeks before every Olympic Games begin, the fire on Mount Olympus which is always burning in Greece — the origins of the Olympic Games — is passed to the official Olympic torch and then begins its journey. Just like a track and field relay, runners reach a destination and then pass off the burning torch to another runner until it reaches the Opening Ceremony stadium.

This year, organizers say the torch will start on May 8th in Marseille, France and then travel to several important locations in France before reaching Paris on July 26th.

However you look at it, it's a long way to travel! Some of these islands were once places that France colonized back in the 1800s. You've got to go to history class to find out more about that!

- The 2024 Olympic Torch Relay will kick off in Marseille, France where a few Olympic games will be hosted later in July and August
- Travel through the most famous (wine) vineyards such as Saint-Emilion in Bordeaux, Chablis in Bourgogne, and Layon in the Loire region
- Then Millau Viaduct (southern France), a feat of civil engineering
- Tavel 7,000km to the Kourou Space Centre in Guyane, a symbol of French and European aerospace excellence
- Surf on the waves of Biarritz (southwestern France) and Teahupo'o (Tahiti)
- Reach Mont Ventoux, the legendary cycling climb in the French Alps
- Visit some older Olympic older venues such as Roland-Garros on the Simonne-Mathieu and the Olympic Aquatics Centre in Saint-Denis and then Stade Yves-du-Manoir in Colombes.

OLYMPIC TORCH SCHEDULE

This is the route the Olympic torch will be taking and when.
Please note the list is not exhaustive of all locations the flame will visit en route.

May 8-9: Marseille
May 10: Toulon
May 11: Manosque
May 12: Arles
May 13: Montpellier
May 14: Bastia
May 15: Perpignan
May 16: Carcassonne
May 17: Toulouse
May 18: Auch
May 19: Tarbes
May 20: Pau
May 22: Périgueux
May 23: Bordeaux
May 24: Angoulême
May 28: Angers
May 29: Laval
May 30: Caen
May 31: Mont Saint-Michel
May 25: Futuroscope
May 27: Châteauroux

June 1: Rennes
June 2: Niort
June 4: Les Sables-d'Olonne
June 5: La Baule
June 6: Vannes
June 7: Brest
June 9: Cayenne (French Guiana)
June 12: Saint-Denis (Réunion)
June 13: Papeete (French Polynesia)
June 15: Baie-Mahault (Guadeloupe)
June 17: Fort-de-France (Martinique)
June 18: Nice
June 19: Avignon
June 20: Valence
June 21: Vichy
June 22: Saint-Étienne
June 23: Chamonix
June 25: Besançon
June 26: Strasbourg
June 27: Metz
June 28: Saint-Dizier
June 29: Verdun
June 30: Reimst

July 2: Lille
July 3: Lens – Liévin
July 4: Amiens
July 5: Le Havre
July 6: Vernon
July 7: Chartres
July 9: Blois
July 10: Orléans
July 11: Auxerre
July 12: Dijon
July 13: Troyes
July 14-15: Paris
July 17: Saintt-Quentin
July 18: Beauvais
July 19: Soisy-sous-Montmorency
July 20: Meaux
July 21: Créteil
July 22: Évry-Courcouronnes
July 23: Versailles
July 24: Esplanade de La Défense, Nanterre
July 25: Parc Georges-Valbon
July 26: Paris — Olympic Games Opening Ceremony

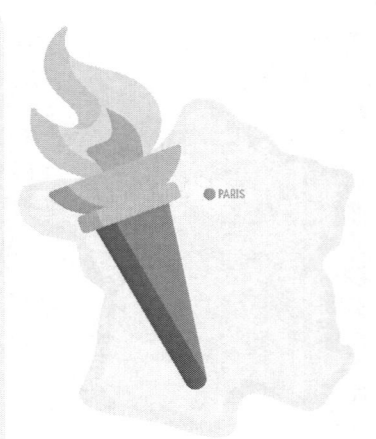

Your assignment: find all these locations on the internet.
https://olympics.com/en/news/paris-2024-olympic-torch-relay-route-unveiled

PARIS 2024 OLYMPICS JOURNAL

Color me!

Paris 2024 Olympics/Shutterstock.com

CIRCLE YOUR TOP 5 FAVORITE SPORTS TO FOLLOW

GOLF	DIVING	TENNIS	WEIGHT LIFTING	ARTISTIC	SPRINT	VOLLEYBALL
ROWING	TRACK CYCLING	RHYTHMIC	WATER POLO	BASKETBALL	ATHLETICS	WRESTLING
TRIATHLON	SHOOTING	SPORT CLIMBING	SWIMMING	RUGBY SEVENS	MOUNTAIN BIKING	BEACH VOLLEYBALL
SAILING	EQUESTRIAN	BREAKING	FENCING	TAEKWONDO	BADMINTON	SLALOM
TABLE TENNIS	ARCHERY	FIELD HOCKEY	MARATHON SWIMMING	ARTISTIC SWIMMING	TRAMPOLINE	BOXING
3X3 BASKETBALL	ROAD CYCLING	CYCLING BMX RACING	SURFING	FOOTBALL	JUDO	HANDBALL
MODERN PENTATHLON	CYCLING BMX FREESTYLE	SKATEBOARDING				

PARIS 2024

Paris 2024 Olympics/Shutterstock.com

12

PARIS 2024 OLYMPICS
WHAT ARE MY TOP 5 FAVORITE SPORTS TO FOLLOW?

NAME

VISIT #1: _____

VISIT #2: _____

VISIT #3: _____

VISIT #4: _____

VISIT #5: _____

Now that you've got your TOP 5 pics — you can journal the winners and which medals they win!

13

WHAT I LIKE ABOUT MY FAVORITE SPORT #1

#1 is my favorite sport because:
___

My favorite thing I saw in this competition was:
___

Something I saw that I've never seen before:
___

Who was the most famous person reporting about it on TV?
___

Something I'm going to tell people about is:
___

Draw and color something below:

SPORT EVENT #1: _____
DATE: _____

TEAM   INDIVIDUAL

PARIS 2024

GOLD

Name: _____

Country: _____

Finishing Time: _____

SILVER

Name: _____

Country: _____

Finishing Time: _____

BRONZE

Name: _____

Country: _____

Finishing Time: _____

Write in your journal in your own words what you experienced, how winning or losing made you feel. Did it inspire you to go out and do some new sports?!

WHAT I LIKE ABOUT MY FAVORITE SPORT #2

#2 is my favorite sport because:

My favorite thing I saw in this competition was:

Something I saw that I've never seen before:

Who was the most famous person reporting about it on TV?

Something I'm going to tell people about is:

Draw and color something below:

SPORT EVENT #2: _____
DATE: _____

☐ TEAM   ☐ INDIVIDUAL

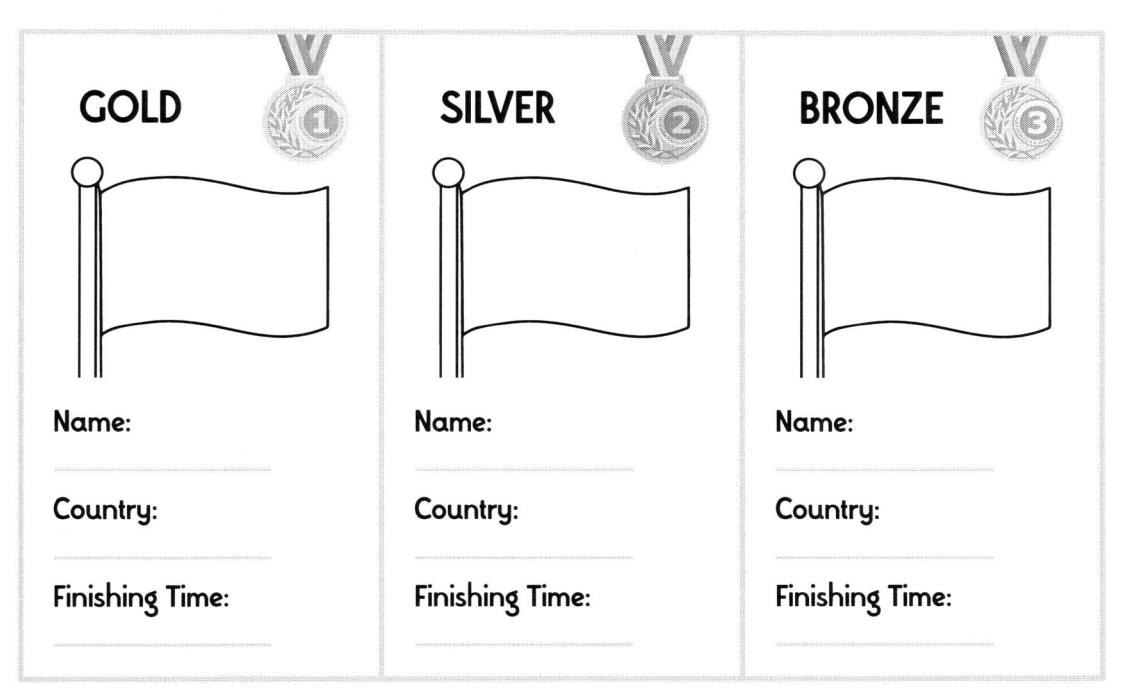

PARIS 2024

GOLD
Name: _____
Country: _____
Finishing Time: _____

SILVER
Name: _____
Country: _____
Finishing Time: _____

BRONZE
Name: _____
Country: _____
Finishing Time: _____

Write in your journal in your own words what you experienced, how winning or losing made you feel. Did it inspire you to go out and do some new sports?!

WHAT I LIKE ABOUT MY FAVORITE SPORT #3

#3 is my favorite sport because:
_____

My favorite thing I saw in this competition was:
_____

Something I saw that I've never seen before:
_____

Who was the most famous person reporting about it on TV?
_____

Something I'm going to tell people about is:
_____

Draw and color something below:

SPORT EVENT #3: _____
DATE: _____

___ TEAM   ___ INDIVIDUAL

PARiS 2024

Paris 2024 Olympics/Shutterstock.com

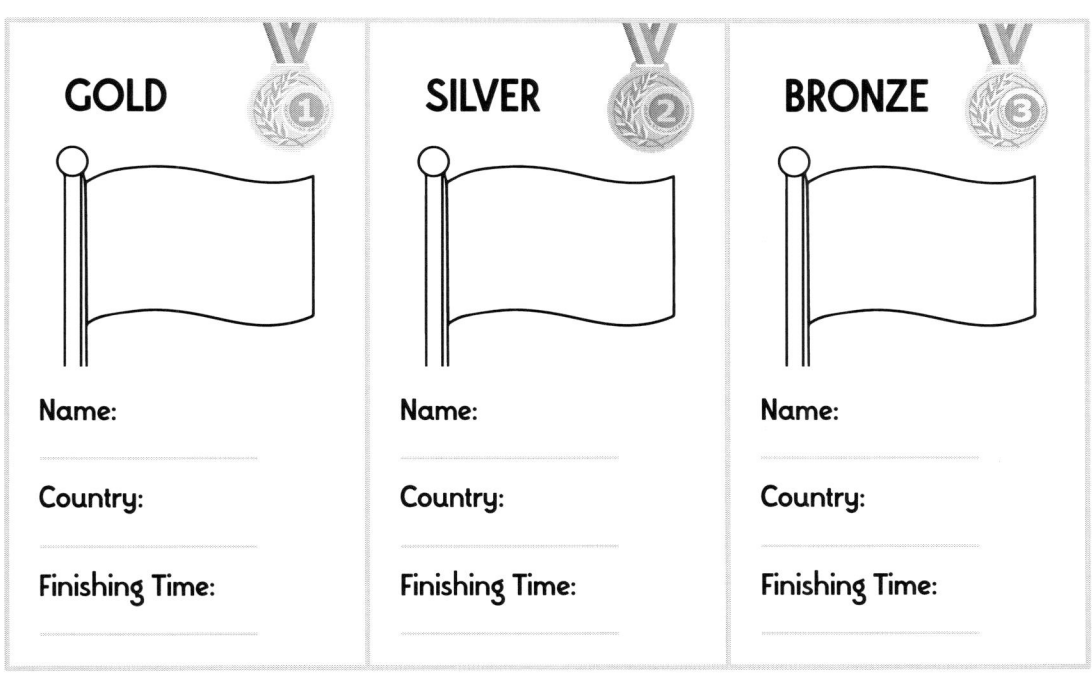

GOLD	SILVER	BRONZE
Name:	Name:	Name:
Country:	Country:	Country:
Finishing Time:	Finishing Time:	Finishing Time:

Write in your journal in your own words what you experienced, how winning or losing made you feel. Did it inspire you to go out and do some new sports?!

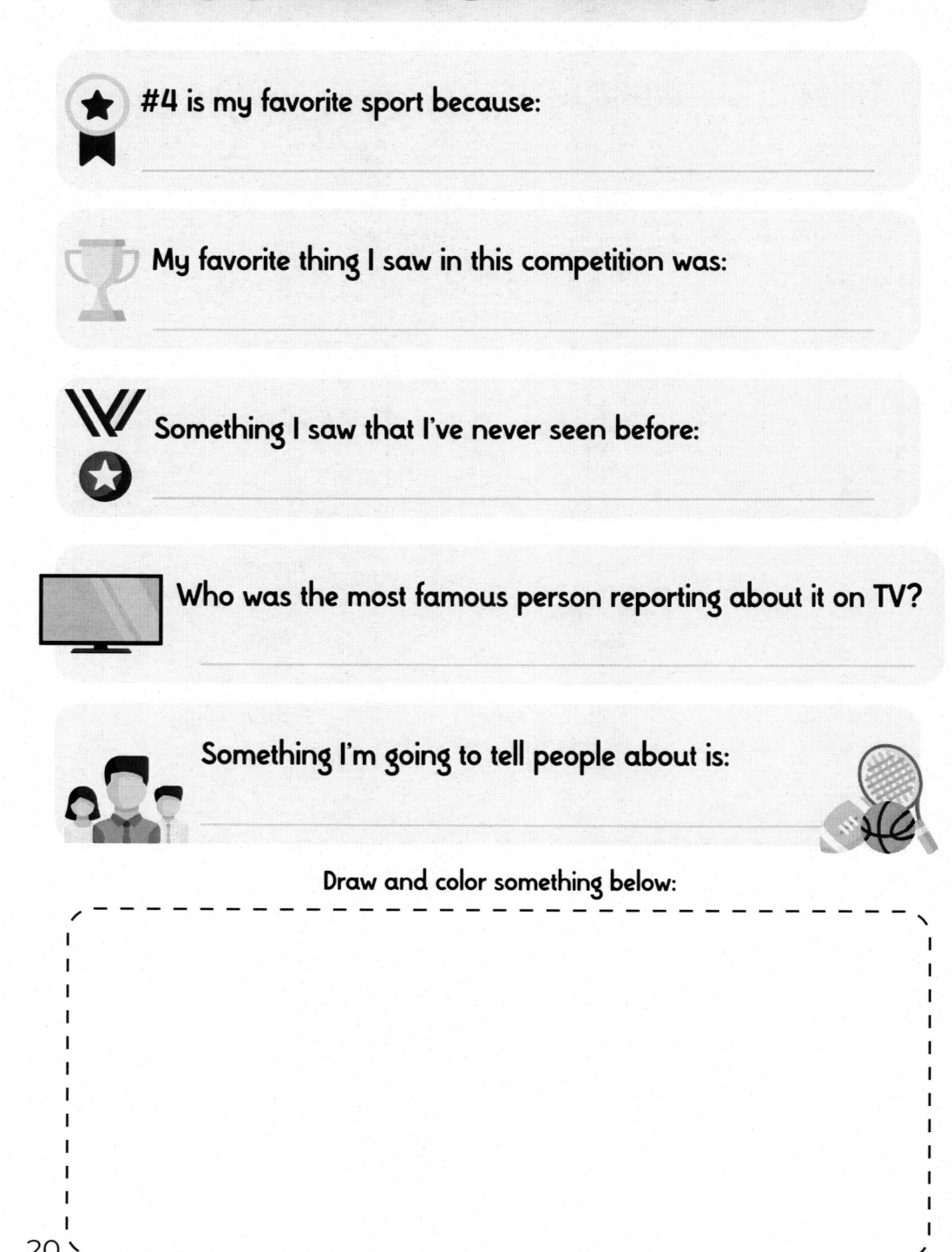

WHAT I LIKE ABOUT MY FAVORITE SPORT #4

#4 is my favorite sport because:
_____

My favorite thing I saw in this competition was:
_____

Something I saw that I've never seen before:
_____

Who was the most famous person reporting about it on TV?
_____

Something I'm going to tell people about is:
_____

Draw and color something below:

SPORT EVENT #4: _____
DATE: _____

☐ TEAM   ☐ INDIVIDUAL

PARIS 2024

Paris 2024 Olympics/Shutterstock.com

GOLD
Name: _____
Country: _____
Finishing Time: _____

SILVER
Name: _____
Country: _____
Finishing Time: _____

BRONZE
Name: _____
Country: _____
Finishing Time: _____

Write in your journal in your own words what you experienced, how winning or losing made you feel. Did it inspire you to go out and do some new sports?!

21

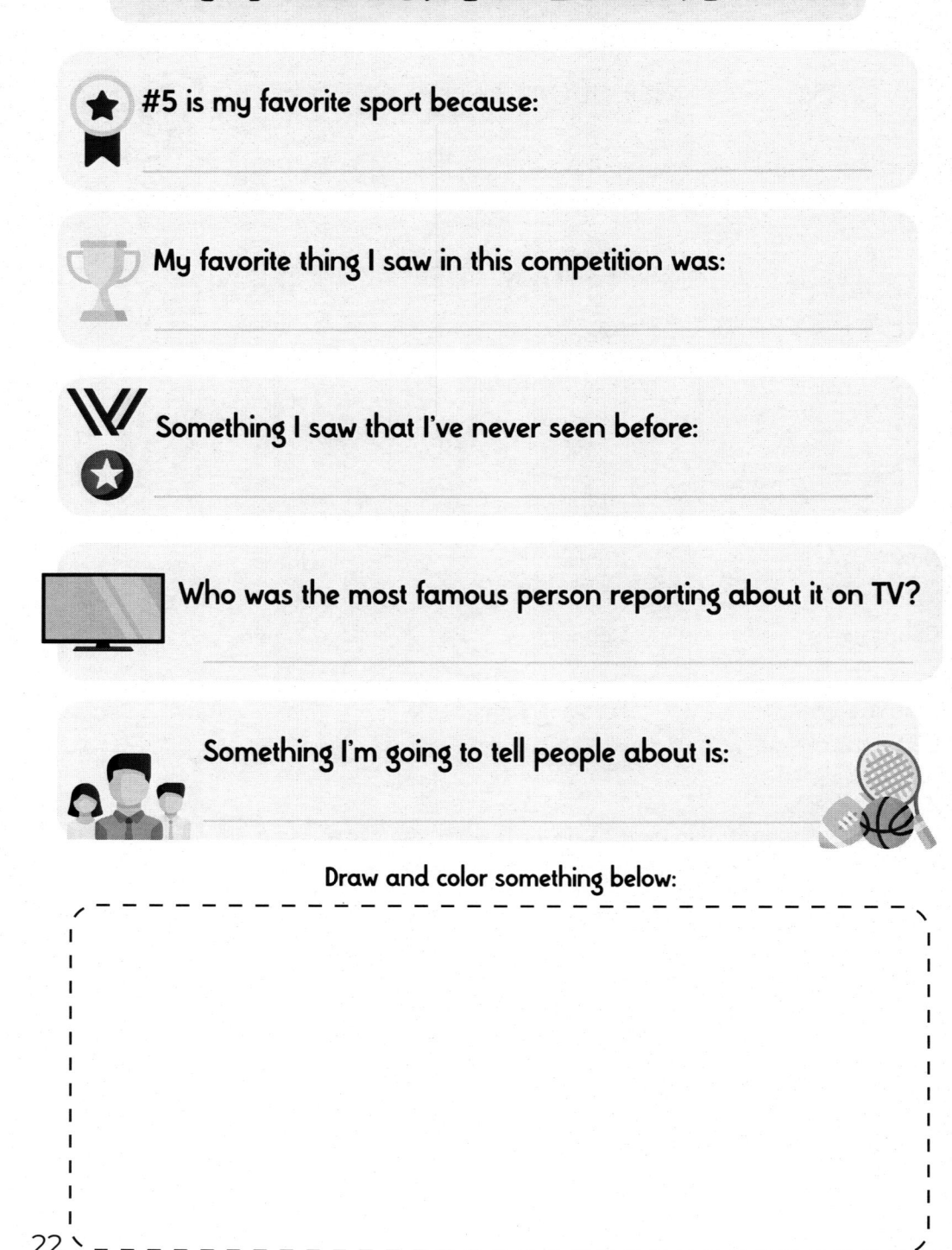

WHAT I LIKE ABOUT MY FAVORITE SPORT #5

#5 is my favorite sport because:
_____

My favorite thing I saw in this competition was:
_____

Something I saw that I've never seen before:
_____

Who was the most famous person reporting about it on TV?
_____

Something I'm going to tell people about is:
_____

Draw and color something below:

SPORT EVENT #5: _____
DATE: _____

TEAM   INDIVIDUAL

PARIS 2024

Paris 2024 Olympics/Shutterstock.com

GOLD

Name: _____

Country: _____

Finishing Time: _____

SILVER

Name: _____

Country: _____

Finishing Time: _____

BRONZE

Name: _____

Country: _____

Finishing Time: _____

Write in your journal in your own words what you experienced, how winning or losing made you feel. Did it inspire you to go out and do some new sports?!

23

WHO ARE YOUR FAVORITE ATHLETES? WHEN ARE THEY COMPETING?

WHO ARE YOUR FAVORITE ATHLETES? WHEN ARE THEY COMPETING?

TOP 15 MEDALISTS BY COUNTRY

Write in your journal in your own words what you experienced, how winning or losing made you feel. Did it inspire you to go out and do some new sports?!

	COUNTRY:	GOLD	SILVER	BRONZE
1.				
2.				
3.				
4.				
5.				
6.				
7.				
8.				
9.				
10.				
11.				
12.				
13.				
14.				
15.				

You can find these stats on the official Olympics website, calendars of events and all the competing countries on Wikipedia too.

PARIS 2024 OLYMPICS

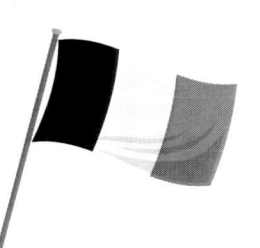

LET THE GAMES BEGIN!

Keep track of what's happening at the Olympic games, watch it on television together. If you write it down, you'll have some great things share with friends and family! And don't forget to ask them what their favorite sports are, too.

Also, get out there and try your favorite sports! You never know, you might be good enough one day to be in the Olympics too!

Andrew & Ashley's EUROPEAN TOURS

KIDS TRAVEL GUIDE TO GERMANY: BAVARIA & MUNICH

Kids' Travel Guide to LONDON!

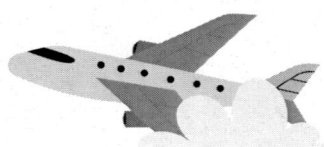

Kids' Cultural Tour of PARIS!

BE SURE TO CHECK OUT THE KIDS' TRAVEL SERIES TAKING YOU TO OTHER CULTURALLY-RICH LOCATIONS!

Get Andrew & Ashley's European Tours Books here.

Manufactured by Amazon.ca
Acheson, AB

13420972R00017